Anal(
Grade

MW01089707

Table of Contents

Introduction

Analogies build critical thinking and reasoning skills that are important in everyday learning as well as for standardized testing. Students can begin to learn the relationships shown in analogies by working with shape analogies and then with picture analogies that compare familiar items. (The Grade 2–3 book in this series introduces shape and picture analogies.) The thinking skills required to complete analogies are creative and higher level, encouraging students to think "out of the box." This kind of reasoning will strengthen their thinking abilities across the curriculum and serve them throughout their lives in all kinds of activities.

ORGANIZATION AND USE

This book is divided into four units: Completing Analogies from a Word Box, Completing Multiple Choice Analogies (One Word), Completing Multiple Choice Analogies (Word Pairs), and Supplying Words to Complete Analogies. The exercises progress from simplest to most difficult, and may be most effective when used in order; however, teachers may use any lesson at any time. Each two-page lesson has a sample exercise and an explanation of how the analogy should be read and completed.

At the end of each lesson is a short "Analogy-Wiz" exercise indicated by the "Wizard" icon. These exercises help stretch students' thinking and prepare them for the types of analogies that are to come in the book. There is also a one-page "Fun with Analogies" lesson at the end of each unit.

Three assessments at the beginning of the book can be used as pre-tests or post-tests, or at any time a teacher wishes to gauge students' understanding of the lessons. The tests cover Completing Analogies from a Word Box, Completing Multiple Choice Analogies, and Supplying Words to Complete Analogies.

On page 3 is an introduction to analogies, which teachers should go over with their students before beginning. The introduction describes what an analogy is, how it looks, and how it should be read. For the fourth and fifth grades, this book has introduced analogies using words, such as "is to" and "as." Later in the book, the symbols ":" and "::" are introduced. Teachers may wish to delay discussion of the symbols until students have had a chance to familiarize themselves with the analogies that use words.

The answer key gives answers as well as relationships to help teachers explain how to think through each analogy.

ADDITIONAL NOTES

Some Analogy-Wiz activities suggest partnering with a classmate or sharing with the class. Additional paper may be required in some cases.

Activities may be completed individually in class or as homework, in small groups or centers, or as a class. It is suggested that the teacher go over the examples and their solutions before having students work independently.

Analogies can be challenging, and they can also be fun. They are, in a sense, puzzles and brain teasers, and students' attitudes toward analogies can be positively influenced by treating the exercises this way. Encourage students to be creative, and be sure to keep an open mind. At times, there will be more than one right answer. If a student has a new answer, ask for an explanation. Through the explanation, the student will more clearly see the error of his or her thinking, or the teacher will see an interesting new solution!

Multiple Choice Analogies

Directions For numbers 11–15, choose the word that best completes each analogy. Darken the circle by the word you choose. Tell why the analogy works, or what it is comparing. The analogies on this page compare numbers, different degrees, or different forms of grammar.

11. <u>sure</u> is to <u>surely</u> **AS** <u>pure</u> is to ?   Ⓐ clear   Ⓑ purity   Ⓒ purely

_____

12. <u>10</u> is to <u>15</u> **AS** <u>20</u> is to ?   Ⓐ 22   Ⓑ 15   Ⓒ 25

_____

13. <u>bad</u> is to <u>worse</u> **AS** <u>good</u> is to ?   Ⓐ better   Ⓑ best   Ⓒ fair

_____

14. <u>15</u> is to <u>45</u> **AS** <u>100</u> is to ?   Ⓐ 25   Ⓑ 200   Ⓒ 300

_____

15. <u>soaked</u> is to <u>damp</u> **AS** <u>freezing</u> is to ?   Ⓐ frozen   Ⓑ cool   Ⓒ frigid

_____

Directions For numbers 16–20, choose the word pair that best completes each analogy. Darken the circle by the word pair you choose.

16. <u>she</u> is to <u>hers</u> **AS** ? is to ?
Ⓐ he / him   Ⓑ he / he's   Ⓒ he / his

17. <u>bright</u> is to <u>brighter</u> **AS** ? is to ?
Ⓐ happy / happiest   Ⓑ happy / joyful   Ⓒ happy / happier

18. <u>12</u> is to <u>3</u> **AS** ? is to ?
Ⓐ 48 / 12   Ⓑ 48 / 4   Ⓒ 48 / 8

19. <u>agree</u> is to <u>disagree</u> **AS** ? is to ?
Ⓐ close / shut   Ⓑ close / disclose   Ⓒ close / slam

20. <u>small</u> is to <u>tiny</u> **AS** ? is to ?
Ⓐ big / tall   Ⓑ big / long   Ⓒ big / huge

Supplying Words

Directions To complete these analogies, you will use words that you already know. Read the first word pair and decide how the two words are related. Then, complete the analogy with a word that will give the second word pair the same relationship. There may be more than one correct answer.

1. picture : art :: song : _____

2. man : woman :: boy : _____

3. spider : web :: _____ : cave

4. birds : flock :: _____ : herd

5. seed : sprout :: sprout : _____

6. chef : cook :: construction worker : _____

7. work : job :: _____ : game

8. ride : bike :: _____ : truck

9. red : color :: _____ : shape

10. breakfast : morning :: supper : _____

11. hockey : sport :: checkers : _____

12. swim : pool :: race : _____

GO ON ⇒

Supplying Words

Directions To complete these analogies, you will use words that you already know. Read the second word pair and decide how the two words are related. Then, complete the analogy with a word that will give the first word pair the same relationship. There may be more than one correct answer.

13. _____ : father :: sister : brother

14. _____ : liquid :: oxygen : gas

15. cat : _____ :: rodent : prey

16. begin : _____ :: finish : complete

17. _____ : chew :: chew : swallow

18. soccer : _____ :: basketball : net

19. dictionary : _____ :: encyclopedia : subjects

20. ruler : _____ :: cup : ounces

21. _____ : Sun :: moon : Earth

22. _____ : sleep :: bathroom : shower

23. _____ : mammal :: snake : reptile

24. _____ : foot :: finger : hand

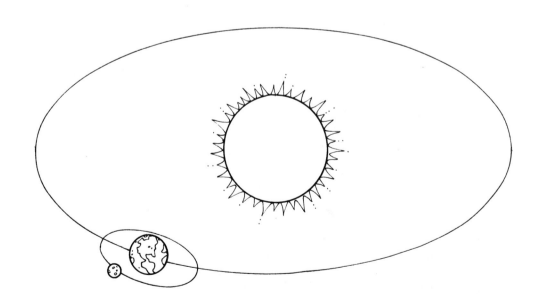

Name _____ Date _____

Opposite or Alike?

An analogy can compare opposites (antonyms) or words that mean almost the same thing (synonyms).

Look at this example:
forward is to backward **AS** upward is to _____   downward   sideward

 Think: How do **forward** and **backward** relate to each other? **Forward** is the opposite direction of **backward**. It is its antonym. Which word is the antonym for **upward**?

Answer: Downward is the antonym for **upward**, so **downward** completes this analogy.

Now look at this example:
instructions are to directions **AS** answers are to _____   questions   solutions

 Think: How do **instructions** and **directions** relate to each other? **Instructions** means almost the same thing as **directions**. These words are synonyms. Which word is a synonym for **answers**?

Answer: Solutions is the synonym for **answers**, so **solutions** completes this analogy.

(Directions) Read each analogy. Decide if the first pair is comparing antonyms or synonyms. Write your choice on the line. Write a word from the box to complete the analogy.

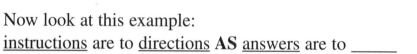

| dry | evening | boredom | sunrise | sorrow |

1. sharp is to dull **AS** happiness is to _____

antonyms or synonyms _____

2. soaked is to wet **AS** parched is to _____

antonyms or synonyms _____

3. dawn is to daybreak **AS** dusk is to _____

antonyms or synonyms _____

GO ON ⇨

Opposite or Alike?

(**Directions**) Read each analogy. Decide if the first pair is comparing antonyms or synonyms. Write your choice on the line. Write a word from the box to complete the analogy.

untrue	success	serious	destroy	weakness	huge
mend	spectacular	threat	strength	remain	tiny

4. <u>brittle</u> is to <u>fragile</u> **AS** <u>wreck</u> is to _____

antonyms or synonyms _____

5. <u>change</u> is to <u>convert</u> **AS** <u>stay</u> is to _____

antonyms or synonyms _____

6. <u>save</u> is to <u>discard</u> **AS** <u>frailty</u> is to _____

antonyms or synonyms _____

7. <u>falter</u> is to <u>hesitate</u> **AS** <u>false</u> is to _____

antonyms or synonyms _____

8. <u>mistake</u> is to <u>correction</u> **AS** <u>failure</u> is to _____

antonyms or synonyms _____

9. <u>safety</u> is to <u>protection</u> **AS** <u>danger</u> is to _____

antonyms or synonyms _____

10. <u>clear</u> is to <u>foggy</u> **AS** <u>ordinary</u> is to _____

antonyms or synonyms _____

11. <u>thaw</u> is to <u>melt</u> **AS** <u>immense</u> is to _____

antonyms or synonyms _____

12. <u>silly</u> is to <u>foolish</u> **AS** <u>sober</u> is to _____

antonyms or synonyms _____

Analogy-Wiz

Write two antonym pairs and two synonym pairs, each on a separate piece of paper. Use the words "is to" between each one. Put your pairs in a bowl with the pairs that the other students have written. Form two teams with class members. Each team takes turns choosing word pairs from the hat to make antonym or synonym analogies.

Rhyme or Rime?

An analogy can compare words that rhyme or words that sound alike but have different spellings and meanings (homophones).

Look at this example:

<u>flour</u> is to <u>hour</u> **AS** <u>carrot</u> is to _____   vegetable   parrot

Think: How do **flour** and **hour** relate to each other? **Flour** rhymes with **hour**. Which word rhymes with **carrot**?

Answer: Parrot rhymes with **carrot**, so **parrot** completes this analogy.

Now look at this example:

<u>flour</u> is to <u>flower</u> **AS** <u>road</u> is to _____   rode   street

Think: How does **flour** relate to **flower**? **Flour** and **flower** are homophones. Which word is a homophone for **road**?

Answer: Rode is the homophone for **road**, so **rode** completes this analogy.

(Directions) Read each analogy. Decide if the first pair is comparing rhyming words or homophones. Write your choice on the line. Write a word from the box to complete the analogy. (Note: Homophones do rhyme, but rhyming words are not always homophones. If the pair is a homophone, choose homophone.)

harden	flew	grew	clasp

1. <u>not</u> is to <u>knot</u> **AS** <u>flu</u> is to _____

   rhyme or homophone _____

2. <u>lamp</u> is to <u>clamp</u> **AS** <u>grasp</u> is to _____

   rhyme or homophone _____

3. <u>park</u> is to <u>stark</u> **AS** <u>garden</u> is to _____

   rhyme or homophone _____

GO ON ⇒

Rhyme or Rime?

Directions Read each analogy. Decide if the first pair is comparing rhyming words or homophones. Write your choice on the line. Write a word from the box to complete the analogy. (Note: Homophones do rhyme, but rhyming words are not always homophones. If the pair is a homophone, choose homophone.)

board	mistake	allowed	thunder	number
flounder	tale	nickel	heaven	flowed

4. <u>too</u> is to <u>two</u> **AS** <u>tail</u> is to _____

   rhyme or homophone _____

5. <u>climb</u> is to <u>slime</u> **AS** <u>pickle</u> is to _____

   rhyme or homophone _____

6. <u>marrow</u> is to <u>barrow</u> **AS** <u>grounder</u> is to _____

   rhyme or homophone _____

7. <u>towed</u> is to <u>toad</u> **AS** <u>bored</u> is to _____

   rhyme or homophone _____

8. <u>knight</u> is to <u>night</u> **AS** <u>aloud</u> is to _____

   rhyme or homophone _____

9. <u>diesel</u> is to <u>weasel</u> **AS** <u>blunder</u> is to _____

   rhyme or homophone _____

10. <u>rubble</u> is to <u>stubble</u> **AS** <u>seven</u> is to _____

    rhyme or homophone _____

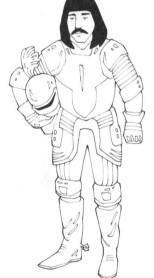

Analogy-Wiz

Write two homophone analogies and two rhyming analogies. Keep the last word of each analogy on a separate piece of paper. Trade analogies with a classmate and solve.

A Piece of the Pie

An analogy can show parts of a whole.

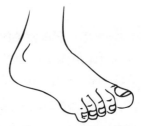

Look at this example:
<u>finger</u> is to <u>hand</u> **AS** <u>toe</u> is to _____   toenail   foot

Think: How do finger and hand relate to each other? A finger is a part of a hand. What is a toe a part of?

Answer: A **toe** is a part of a **foot**, so **foot** completes this analogy.

(Directions) Read each analogy. Decide in what way the first pair shows a part of a whole. Choose a word from the box that shows the same type of relationship, and write it on the line to complete the analogy.

tree	book	steel	downtown
soft	writer	leg	coyote

1. <u>feather</u> is to <u>bird</u> **AS** <u>fur</u> is to _____

2. <u>tent</u> is to <u>campground</u> **AS** <u>skyscraper</u> is to _____

3. <u>nose</u> is to <u>face</u> **AS** <u>knee</u> is to _____

4. <u>paragraph</u> is to <u>story</u> **AS** <u>page</u> is to _____

5. <u>blossom</u> is to <u>petal</u> **AS** <u>leaf</u> is to _____

(GO ON ⇒)

A Piece of the Pie

(**Directions**) Read each analogy. Decide in what way the first pair shows a part of a whole. Choose a word from the box that shows the same type of relationship, and write it on the line to complete the analogy.

pillow	television	galaxy	sentence	couch	races	pen
shirt	automobile	sled	century	night	hole	elephant

6. antler is to deer **AS** tusk is to _____

7. wheels are to bicycle **AS** runners are to _____

8. latch is to door **AS** button is to _____

9. rudder is to boat **AS** steering wheel is to _____

10. mouse is to computer **AS** remote control is to _____

11. lead is to pencil **AS** ink is to _____

12. mattress is to bed **AS** cushion is to _____

13. letters are to alphabet **AS** words are to _____

14. months are to year **AS** years are to _____

15. grain of sand is to beach **AS** star is to _____

Analogy-Wiz

These analogies use symbols instead of words.
: means **is to**, and :: means **AS**.

Draw a line to connect each analogy to the word that completes it.

wings : moth :: legs :   ship

cockpit : airplane :: bridge :   thermometer

hands : clock :: mercury :   human

Name _____ Date _____

Causing an Effect

An analogy can describe a cause and an effect.

Look at this example:
<u>tired</u> is to <u>rest</u> **AS** <u>hungry</u> is to _____   meal   eat

Think: How do **tired** and **rest** relate to each other? Because you are tired, you rest. Being tired is the cause, and resting is the effect. What would be the effect of being hungry?

Answer: Because you are **hungry**, you **eat**, so **eat** completes this analogy.

(**Directions**) Read each analogy. Look at the first word pair. Which word is the cause? What is the effect? Choose a word from the box that shows the same type of relationship, and write it on the line to complete the analogy.

weakness	hard	distrust	soothe
occupation	earn	bright	dry

1. <u>water</u> is to <u>wet</u> **AS** <u>sun</u> is to _____

2. <u>bump</u> is to <u>hurt</u> **AS** <u>rub</u> is to _____

3. <u>study</u> is to <u>learn</u> **AS** <u>work</u> is to _____

4. <u>exercise</u> is to <u>strength</u> **AS** <u>laziness</u> is to _____

5. <u>honesty</u> is to <u>trust</u> **AS** <u>lies</u> are to _____

(GO ON ⇨)

Causing an Effect

(Directions) Read each analogy. Look at the first word pair. Which word is the cause? What is the effect? Choose a word from the box that shows the same type of relationship, and write it on the line to complete the analogy.

quiet	escape	tornado	cure	doctor	approach
truth	tears	calm	wither	fiction	confusion

6. communication is to understanding **AS** silence is to _____

7. clouds are to rainstorm **AS** winds are to _____

8. shout is to frighten **AS** whisper is to _____

9. happiness is to laughter **AS** sorrow is to _____

10. care is to flourish **AS** neglect is to _____

11. ship is to seasick **AS** medicine is to _____

12. pursue is to capture **AS** flee is to _____

Analogy-Wiz

These analogies use symbols instead of words. Draw a line to connect each analogy to the word that completes it.

success : confidence :: failure :   still

search : find :: misplace :   hesitation

restless : move :: sleepy :   lose

Analogy Crossword

(**Directions**) To complete this crossword, you will first need to complete the analogies. These are a mix of all the different types of analogies in Unit One. More than one word may work in the analogy, but only one word will work in the crossword. Your challenge is to find the word that works in both places. To help you out, every letter *s* is already in the puzzle.

DOWN

1. uncertain is to unsure **AS** shy is to _____
3. rude is to polite **AS** noisy is to _____
4. fruit is to suit **AS** since is to _____
5. bureau is to drawer **AS** cupboard is to _____
7. flee is to flea **AS** to is to _____

ACROSS

2. senseless is to silly **AS** sensible is to _____
6. kindness is to reward **AS** crime is to _____
8. questions are to answers **AS** problems are to _____

What's It Like?

An analogy can compare things by describing their color or size, how they feel or look, what they sound like, or other characteristics.

Look at this example:
tree is to tall **AS** shrub is to ?   green   short

Think: How do **tree** and **tall** relate to each other? **Tall** describes the size of a **tree**. Which word describes the size of a **shrub**?

Answer: Short describes the size of a **shrub**, so **short** completes this analogy.

(**Directions**) Read each analogy. Decide what the relationship is in the first pair. In what way is something being described? Circle the word that completes the analogy. Write what the relationship is.

1. hoop is to circle **AS** globe is to ?   sphere   Earth

_____

2. scissors are to sharp **AS** spoon is to ?   eat   rounded

_____

3. rainbow is to colorful **AS** road is to ?   cars   dull

_____

4. brick is to rough **AS** glass is to ?   fragile   smooth

_____

5. fireworks are to loud **AS** chess is to ?   quiet   difficult

_____

6. desert is to dry **AS** rain forest is to ?   dark   humid

_____   (GO ON ⇨)

What's It Like?

Directions Read each analogy. Decide what the relationship is in the first pair. In what way is something being described? Circle the word that completes the analogy.

7. <u>alley</u> is to <u>narrow</u> **AS** <u>highway</u> is to ?   wide   busy

_____

8. <u>valley</u> is to <u>low</u> **AS** <u>mountain</u> is to ?   high   enormous

_____

9. <u>turtle</u> is to <u>sluggish</u> **AS** <u>cheetah</u> is to ?   fleet   sinewy

_____

10. <u>silk</u> is to <u>smooth</u> **AS** <u>sandpaper</u> is to ?   wood   rough

_____

11. <u>ocean</u> is to <u>deep</u> **AS** <u>pond</u> is to ?   shallow   murky

_____

12. <u>jack hammer</u> is to <u>jolting</u> **AS** <u>painting</u> is to ?   brush   smooth

_____

13. <u>jalapeño</u> is to <u>spicy</u> **AS** <u>rice</u> is to ?   bland   white

_____

14. <u>powder</u> is to <u>satiny</u> **AS** <u>sand</u> is to ?   gritty   tiny

_____

15. <u>encyclopedia</u> is to <u>heavy</u> **AS** <u>pamphlet</u> is to ?   thin   light

_____

Analogy-Wiz

Write three describing analogies. Use the symbols : and :: instead of the words **is to** and **AS**.

_____

_____

_____

Different Degrees

An analogy can compare words by describing different degrees of the same thing.

Look at this example:
<u>pretty</u> is to <u>gorgeous</u> **AS** <u>tired</u> is to ?   sleepy   exhausted

Think: How do **pretty** and **gorgeous** relate to each other? Both words describe degrees of beauty, and **gorgeous** is the most beautiful. Which word describes the most tired?

Answer: Sleepy is **tired**, but **exhausted** is the most **tired**, so **exhausted** completes this analogy.

Now look at this example:
<u>warm</u> is to <u>hot</u> **AS** <u>cold</u> is to ?   freezing   cool

Think: How do **warm** and **hot** relate to each other? Both words describe degrees of warmth, and **hot** is very warm. Which word describes very cold?

Answer: Cool is a degree of **cold**, but **freezing** is very **cold**, so **freezing** completes this analogy.

(**Directions**) Read each analogy. Decide what the relationship is in the first pair. Circle the word that completes the analogy.

1. <u>smart</u> is to <u>brilliant</u> **AS** <u>scared</u> is to ?   terrified   worried

2. <u>old</u> is to <u>antique</u> **AS** <u>hungry</u> is to ?   food   starving

3. <u>big</u> is to <u>enormous</u> **AS** <u>small</u> is to ?   little   tiny

GO ON ⇨

Different Degrees

Directions Read each analogy. Decide what the relationship is in the first pair. Circle the word that completes the analogy.

4. far is to distant **AS** near is to ?   here   close

5. inexpensive is to free **AS** valuable is to ?   priceless   expensive

6. furious is to angry **AS** thrilled is to ?   worried   happy

7. sad is to mournful **AS** silly is to ?   ridiculous   funny

8. rotten is to bad **AS** delicious is to ?   soft   tasty

9. presentation is to spectacle **AS** bad is to ?   mean   evil

10. important is to urgent **AS** strange is to ?   unbelievable   odd

11. tragedy is to trouble **AS** breathtaking is to ?   ugly   pretty

12. chat is to discussion **AS** think is to ?   decide   analyze

13. troublemaker is to criminal **AS** smart is to ?   genius   intelligent

14. trickle is to gush **AS** sniffle is to ?   bawl   cry

15. miserable is to sad **AS** ecstatic is to ?   extreme   happy

Analogy-Wiz

These analogies use symbols instead of words. Write a degree word to complete each analogy.

good : best :: bad : _____

big : massive :: small : _____

special : extraordinary :: great : _____

Name _____ Date _____

Grammar-Time

An analogy can compare different forms of words.

Look at this example:

go is to went **AS** fly is to ?

   Ⓐ flyer   Ⓑ flew   Ⓒ flying

Think: How do **go** and **went** relate to each other? **Went** is the past tense of **go**. Which word is the past tense of **fly**?

Answer: Flew is the past tense of **fly**, so **flew** completes this analogy. Darken the circle by **flew**.

(Directions) Read each analogy. Decide how the two words in the first pair compare grammatically. Choose the word that compares in the same way with the third word to complete the analogy. Darken the circle next to your choice.

1. she is to he **AS** hers is to ?

   Ⓐ him   Ⓑ he   Ⓒ his

2. my is to mine **AS** your is to ?

   Ⓐ yours   Ⓑ you   Ⓒ our

3. drank is to drink **AS** ran is to ?

   Ⓐ running   Ⓑ runs   Ⓒ run

4. sleepy is to sleepier **AS** wavy is to ?

   Ⓐ waver   Ⓑ wavier   Ⓒ waves

5. think is to thought **AS** bring is to ?

   Ⓐ bringing   Ⓑ brings   Ⓒ brought

(GO ON ⟹)

Grammar-Time

(**Directions**) Read each analogy. Decide how the two words in the first pair compare grammatically. Choose the word that compares in the same way with the third word to complete the analogy. Darken the circle next to your choice.

6. it is to its **AS** they is to ?
   Ⓐ they're   Ⓑ their   Ⓒ there

7. call is to caller **AS** dance is to ?
   Ⓐ dancer   Ⓑ dancers   Ⓒ danced

8. stand is to stood **AS** sit is to ?
   Ⓐ sat   Ⓑ sits   Ⓒ sitting

9. carver is to carving **AS** painter is to ?
   Ⓐ picture   Ⓑ painting   Ⓒ paints

10. me is to mine **AS** she is to ?
   Ⓐ her   Ⓑ hers   Ⓒ she

11. rush is to rushing **AS** drive is to ?
   Ⓐ driver   Ⓑ driving   Ⓒ drives

12. is is to was **AS** are is to ?
   Ⓐ were   Ⓑ aren't   Ⓒ a

13. heavy is to heaviest **AS** wet is to ?
   Ⓐ wetter   Ⓑ soaked   Ⓒ wettest

14. swimmer is to swam **AS** runner is to ?
   Ⓐ run   Ⓑ running   Ⓒ ran

15. measurement is to measure **AS** discussion is to ?
   Ⓐ discussed   Ⓑ discuss   Ⓒ discussing

16. height is to heighten **AS** bright is to ?
   Ⓐ brighter   Ⓑ brightest   Ⓒ brighten

Analogy-Wiz

    Write two grammar analogies using the symbols : and :: instead of the words **is to** and **AS**. Write what your analogies are comparing. Share your analogies with your class.

numeric-alogies

An analogy can compare relationships between numbers. Relationships may be found through addition, subtraction, multiplication, or division. An analogy can use symbols instead of words. : means **is to** and :: means **AS**.

Look at this example:

2 : 4 :: 6 : ?

Ⓐ 7   Ⓑ 12   Ⓒ 3

Think: What is the relationship between **2** and **4**? Or, what do you need to do to 2 to get 4? **4** is twice as much as **2**. Which number is twice as much as 6?

Answer: 12 is twice as much as 6, so **12** completes this analogy. Darken the circle for **12**.

Now look at this example:

7 : 21 :: 4 : ?

Ⓐ 12   Ⓑ 16   Ⓒ 20

Think: What is the relationship between **7** and **21**? Or, what do you need to do to 7 to get 21? 3 times **7** equals **21**. Which number is 3 times 4?

Answer: 12 is 3 times 4, so **12** completes this analogy. Darken the circle for **12**.

(Directions) Look at the first pair of numbers in each analogy. Decide what their relationship is. Darken the circle by the number that shows the same relationship for the second pair.

1. 9 : 10 :: 14 : ?

Ⓐ 11   Ⓑ 15   Ⓒ 7

2. 2 : 6 :: 5 : ?

Ⓐ 10   Ⓑ 3   Ⓒ 15

(GO ON ⇒)

Numeric-alogies

Directions Look at the first pair of numbers in each analogy. Decide what their relationship is. Darken the circle by the number that shows the same relationship for the second pair.

3. 31 : 36 :: 53 : ?
   Ⓐ 58   Ⓑ 56   Ⓒ 48

4. 300 : 150 :: 50 : ?
   Ⓐ 100   Ⓑ 25   Ⓒ 0

5. 42 : 28 :: 33 : ?
   Ⓐ 19   Ⓑ 22   Ⓒ 15

6. 5 : 20 :: 3 : ?
   Ⓐ 12   Ⓑ 9   Ⓒ 1

7. 11 : 13 :: 0 : ?
   Ⓐ 11   Ⓑ 2   Ⓒ 3

8. 9 : 9 :: 1 : ?
   Ⓐ 9   Ⓑ 0   Ⓒ 1

9. 30 : 40 :: 50 : ?
   Ⓐ 60   Ⓑ 70   Ⓒ 20

10. 150 : 300 :: 250 : ?
   Ⓐ 350   Ⓑ 100   Ⓒ 500

11. 0 : 0 :: 99 : ?
   Ⓐ 100   Ⓑ 0   Ⓒ 99

12. 36 : 6 :: 72 : ?
   Ⓐ 12   Ⓑ 9   Ⓒ 36

Analogy-Wiz

Write a number analogy on a small index card, then cut the analogy in two pieces. Label one desk or area **A** and one desk or area **B**. Place half your analogy on A and the other half on B, face up. Form two teams with class members. Each team should take turns choosing pairs from A and B that go together to make an analogy. Read your number pairs to the class. If they agree that it is a true analogy, your team gets a point. Place correct analogies in a pile for your team.

Analogy Scramble

(**Directions**) Read each analogy. Unscramble the answer choices. Write the correct answer on the lines. (There may be more lines than you need.) Then, use the letters in the boxes to make a new word that will complete the mystery analogy.

1. <u>dancer</u> is to <u>graceful</u> **AS** <u>artist</u> is to ?   ticreeva   retnpia

⬜ ___ ___ ___ ___ ___ ___ ___ ___

2. <u>he</u> is to <u>him</u> **AS** <u>they</u> is to ?   mthe   erhte

___ ___ ___ ⬜ ___ ___ ___

3. <u>thirty-three</u> is to <u>eleven</u> **AS** <u>ninety-nine</u> is to ?   einn   irtthy-reeth

___ ___ ⬜ ___ ___ ___ ___ ___ ___ ___

4. <u>some</u> is to <u>all</u> **AS** <u>few</u> is to ?   enno   lraesev

⬜ ___ ___ ___ ___ ___ ___ ___

5. <u>cheetah</u> is to <u>fast</u> **AS** <u>mountain goat</u> is to ?   blimen   latl

___ ___ ___ ⬜ ___ ___ ___ ___ ___

6. <u>nine</u> is to <u>two</u> **AS** <u>twelve</u> is to ?   xsi   evif

___ ___ ⬜ ___ ___

7. <u>crocodile</u> is to <u>jaws</u> **AS** <u>eagle</u> is to ?   fwsit   alonst

___ ⬜ ___ ___

8. <u>four</u> is to <u>eight</u> **AS** <u>seven</u> is to ?   elvwte   veenle

___ ⬜ ___ ___ ___ ___

Mystery Analogy:

<u>pieces</u> are to <u>puzzle</u> **AS** <u>words</u> are to ?   ____ ____ ____ ____ ____ ____ ____ ____

Group Thinking

An analogy can compare members of different groups.
Sometimes, you will need to choose a word pair to complete an analogy.

Look at this example:
fish : school ::   book : library   bird : flock

Think: How do the words in the first pair compare to each other? Fish swim in a school. It is how they travel. Which word pair is most like the first?

Answer: A book is a part of a library, but it does not travel with it. It is not living. A bird flies in a flock. Birds and fish are both animals. In this way, bird : flock is more like fish : school. So **bird : flock** completes this analogy.

(**Directions**) Read each word pair. Write the letter of the pair in the second column that is most closely related to a pair in the first column.

_____ **1.** man : men ::   **a.** turtle : amphibians

_____ **2.** star : galaxy ::   **b.** whale : pod

_____ **3.** student : class ::   **c.** surgeon : doctors

_____ **4.** elephant : herd ::   **d.** woman : women

_____ **5.** snake : reptiles ::   **e.** planet : solar system

_____ **6.** woodworker :: craftspeople ::   **f.** worker : crew

(GO ON ⇒)

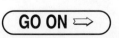

Group Thinking

(Directions) Read each word pair. Write the letter of the pair in the second column that is most closely related to a pair in the first column.

_____ **7.** sun : stars ::

_____ **8.** plate : dishes ::

_____ **9.** dog : pack ::

_____ **10.** wolf : mammals ::

_____ **11.** pie : desserts ::

_____ **12.** soccer : sports ::

_____ **13.** notebook : school supplies ::

_____ **14.** iron : metals ::

_____ **15.** cinnamon : spices ::

_____ **16.** house : neighborhood ::

g. spoon : silverware

h. fly : insects

i. quartz : minerals

j. casserole : dinners

k. Earth : planets

l. office : business park

m. cow : herd

n. wheat : grains

o. speed skater : athletes

p. building blocks : toys

Analogy-Wiz

Write two word pairs to begin two different group analogies. Trade your word pairs with a classmate to finish.

Habits and Habitats

An analogy may compare things according to what they do or where they live. You will compare word pairs to complete these analogies.

Look at this example:
fox : den ::   bird : fly   bird : nest

Think: How do **fox** and **den** relate to each other? A den is where a fox lives. Which analogy pair describes where something lives?

Answer: Fly describes what a **bird** does. **Nest** describes where a **bird** lives, so **bird** : **nest** completes this analogy.

(Directions) **Read each analogy pair. Read the choices to complete the analogy. Circle the word pair that relates to each other the way that the first pair does.**

1. elephant : walk ::   snake : slither   gopher : prairie

2. polar bear : arctic ::   flamingo : flock   toucan : rain forest

3. whale : migrate ::   bear : hibernate   bear : mammal

4. bear : den ::   bird : sky   bee : hive

5. raccoon : omnivore ::   lion : pride   lion : carnivore

6. jellyfish : ocean ::   deer : forest   blue jay : sky

(GO ON ⇒)

Habits and Habitats

Directions Read each analogy pair. Read the choices to complete the analogy. Circle the word pair that relates to each other the way that the first pair does.

7. alligator : swamp ::   bison : plains   bison : horns

8. fish : scales ::   ostrich : bird   bird : feathers

9. chameleon : camouflage ::   snake : venom   snake : den

10. ram : horns ::   walrus : tusks   walrus : arctic

11. elk : speed ::   penguin : snow   rhinoceros : horn

12. desert rat : desert ::   walrus : tusks   walrus : arctic

13. Canada goose : migrate ::   seal : ocean   toad : hibernate

14. school : fish ::   swarm : bee   ocean : dolphin

15. lion : stealth ::   eagle : flight   eagle : speed

Analogy-Wiz

Write two word pairs to begin two different group analogies. Trade your word pairs with a classmate to finish. Share your word pairs with the class. Talk about why they make good analogies.

What's It For?

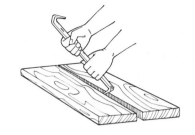

An analogy can compare what things are for, what they do, or how we use them.

Look at the example:

staple : attach ::   hammer : nail   crowbar : separate

Think: A staple is used to attach things. Which of the word pairs describes what something is used for?

Answer: The **crowbar** is used to **separate** things, so **crowbar** : **separate** completes this analogy.

(**Directions**) **Read each word pair. Decide what the relationship is between the words. Circle the word pair that shows the same relationship as the first word pair.**

1. tape : stick ::   paper clip : metal   scissors : cut

2. sun : shine ::   shade : darkness   moon : glow

3. water : wet ::   towel : dry   dew : morning

4. green : go ::   clock : time   red : stop

5. heat : spoil ::   ice : preserve   ice : cold

(GO ON ⇨)

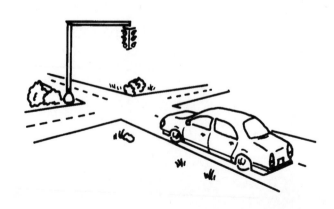

Name _____ Date _____

What's It For?

(**Directions**) The word pairs on this page compare things that have similar uses. Read each word pair. Circle the word pair that describes the same, or a similar, action to the first word pair.

6. fire : burn ::	heat : warm	iron : clothes
7. teacher : teach ::	student : learn	professor : instruct
8. knife : slice ::	saw : cut	spoon : stir
9. puzzle : assemble ::	game : play	mystery : solve
10. hand : press ::	cutter : shape	rolling pin : roll
11. train : transport ::	ship : carry	car : drive
12. roof : shelter ::	house : live	umbrella : protect
13. charcoal : draw ::	pencil : write	artist : paint
14. button : push ::	pedal : press	handle : pull

Analogy-Wiz

Write analogies comparing what things are for, what they do, and how we use them. Share your analogies with the class. When one is read aloud, the rest of the class should say what kind of analogy it is.

Name _____ Date _____

What Do They Do?

An analogy can describe what things or people do.
This exercise compares similar word pairs.

Look at the example.
falcon : fly ::

Ⓐ shark : swim   Ⓑ shark : ocean   Ⓒ shark : fish

Think: What is the relationship between **falcon** and **fly**? A falcon flies to move around. Which word pair describes how something moves?

Answer: A **shark** moves by swimming. So **shark** : **swim** completes this analogy. Darken the circle for shark : swim.

(Directions) Read each word pair. Decide what the relationship is between the words. Choose a pair that shows the same relationship. Darken the circle by the word pair you choose.

1. architect : design ::
   Ⓐ chef : cook   Ⓑ wolf : howl   Ⓒ boxer : strong

2. astronaut : space ::
   Ⓐ ship : cargo   Ⓑ captain : crew   Ⓒ astronomer : sky

3. apprentice : learn ::
   Ⓐ master : teach   Ⓑ student : books   Ⓒ teacher : plans

GO ON ⇒

What Do They Do?

(**Directions**) Read each word pair. Decide what the relationship is between the words. Choose a pair that shows the same relationship. Darken the circle by the word pair you choose.

4. coyote : hunt ::
    Ⓐ gazelle : run   Ⓑ spider : trap   Ⓒ dog : pack

5. violin : music ::
    Ⓐ bell : chime   Ⓑ camera : film   Ⓒ picture : frame

6. comedy : laughter ::
    Ⓐ ball : bounce   Ⓑ thriller : fright   Ⓒ novel : read

7. surgeon : operate ::
    Ⓐ baker : bread   Ⓑ clown : funny   Ⓒ lawyer : defend

8. florist : flowers ::
    Ⓐ farmer : crops   Ⓑ ballerina : toe shoes   Ⓒ ball player : fans

9. carpenter : cabinets ::
    Ⓐ teacher : class   Ⓑ photographer : photos   Ⓒ doctor : hospital

10. sugar : sweeten ::
    Ⓐ cereal : milk   Ⓑ pickle : sour   Ⓒ salt : season

Analogy-Wiz

       Work with a classmate. Use one piece of paper and the symbols : and :: to write your analogy. The first person writes the first word of an analogy, then passes the paper to his or her partner. The second person writes the next word and passes it back to the first person. Now the first person needs to write the third word of the analogy and pass it back again. The second person writes the last word. Try to write a true analogy. Remember, there are many ways to make an analogy work, and the analogy may be as silly as you like, as long as it is true. Share your analogy with your class.

Analogy Pair Challenge

Directions Read each word pair describing what things or people do. Decide what the relationship is between the words. Find the word pair in the second column whose relationship most closely resembles it. Write the letter of the word pair you choose on the line by the first pair.

_____ **1.** hammer : pound ::   **a.** dancer : ballet

_____ **2.** baby : cry ::   **b.** jewelry : decorate

_____ **3.** mime : expression ::   **c.** thermometer : temperature

_____ **4.** phone : ring ::   **d.** wrench : turn

_____ **5.** textbook : teach ::   **e.** radiator : heat

_____ **6.** hydrant : water ::   **f.** utility pole : electricity

_____ **7.** actor : play ::   **g.** clock : chime

_____ **8.** clock : time ::   **h.** actor : lines

_____ **9.** clothing : cover ::   **i.** fiction : entertain

_____ **10.** fan : cool ::   **j.** boy : talk

Double-Cross

(Directions) To complete this crossword, first complete each analogy by choosing the correct pair from the box. Then, put each word pair answer into the crossword. (Hint: The dark bars show where one word in the pair ends, and the next begins.)

1. bee : swarm ::
2. shark : ocean ::
3. keys : strike ::
4. gumdrop : candy ::
5. peas : pod ::
6. chair : sit ::

Word Pair Answer Box
puzzle : pieces
bird : flock
desert rat : desert
rug : floor
punchline : joke
bed : lie
corn : husk
whale : mammal
cookie : dessert
strings : strum
arctic hare : camouflage
instrument : music

First Things First

To complete these analogies, you will need to supply the last word. You will use words that you already know. These analogies relate to sequence—the order in which things happen or when they happen.

Look at this example:
morning : breakfast :: evening : _____

Think: How do **morning** and **breakfast** relate to each other? **Morning** is the time when people usually eat breakfast. What word tells what people usually eat in the evening?

Answer: People usually eat **supper** in the **evening**, so **supper** completes this analogy.

Now look at this example:
wake : rise :: lie down : _____

Think: How do **wake** and **rise** relate to each other? After we wake, we rise from our beds. What happens after we lie down?

Answer: After we **lie down**, we usually **sleep**, so **sleep** completes this analogy.

Directions Read each analogy. Decide what the relationship is in the first word pair. (Remember, order is important.) Then, complete the analogy with a word that has the same relationship with the third word.

1. open : enter :: close : _____

2. wake : morning :: sleep : _____

3. crawl : walk :: walk : _____

4. leave : pack :: return : _____

GO ON ⇨

First Things First

Directions Read each analogy. Decide what the relationship is in the first word pair. (Remember, order is important.) Then, complete the analogy with a word that has the same relationship with the third word.

5. plant : grow :: pick : _____

6. chick : hen :: calf : _____

7. study : learn :: learn : _____

8. Sunday : Monday :: Friday : _____

9. bite : chew :: chew : _____

10. reach : grasp :: grasp : _____

11. smile : laugh :: frown : _____

12. sit : rest :: stand : _____

13. January : February :: August : _____

14. drop : break :: break : _____

15. cook : eat :: pour : _____

Analogy-Wiz

With a partner, think of a sequence analogy. Take turns acting out each word of your analogy for your class. Do not use words. Use the space below to draw your analogy.

Name _____ Date _____

The Second Word

To complete these analogies, you will need to supply the second word.
These analogies relate to what things do, describe things, or compare groups.

Look at this example:
postal worker : _____ :: sanitation truck : take away

Think: What is the relationship between the words in the second word pair? **Take away** is what a **sanitation truck** does to your trash. What does a **postal worker** do?

Answer: A **postal worker delivers** your mail, so **deliver** completes this analogy.

Now look at this example:
Sun : _____ :: grass : green

Think: What is the relationship between the words in the second word pair? **Green** is the color of **grass**. What is the color of the **Sun**?

Answer: The Sun is usually yellow, so **yellow** completes this analogy.

(**Directions**) Read the words in the second word pair. Decide what their relationship is. Then, think of a word with the same, or a similar, relationship to the first word. Write it on the line.

1. green : _____ :: rectangle : shape

2. mother : _____ :: brother : sibling

3. checkers : _____ :: engineering : occupation

4. suspense : _____ :: comedy : funny

(GO ON ⇨)

The Second Word

Directions Read the words in the second word pair. Decide what their relationship is. Then, think of a word with the same, or a similar, relationship to the first word. Write it on the line.

5. potato : _____ :: peach : fruit

6. oxygen : _____ :: ice : solid

7. Pacific : _____ :: Australia : continent

8. Earth : _____ :: Sun : star

9. ball : _____ :: brick : rectangular

10. leopard : _____ :: house cat : tame

11. beagle : _____ :: Siamese : cat

12. wheat : _____ :: cotton : fabric

13. flower : _____ :: horse : animal

14. bee : _____ :: snake : reptile

15. smell : _____ :: heart : organ

Analogy-Wiz

Write two analogies that describe things. Leave out the second word. Trade analogies with a classmate to complete.

_____ : _____ :: _____ : _____

_____ : _____ :: _____ : _____

Name _____   Date _____

The Third Word

To complete these analogies, you will need to supply the third word. These analogies describe causes and effects.

Look at this example:
tired : sleep :: _____ : eat

Think: What is the relationship between the words in the first word pair? When we are **tired**, we **sleep**. What causes us to eat?

Answer: We **eat** when we are **hungry**, so **hungry** completes this analogy.

(Directions) **Read the words in the first word pair. Decide which is the cause and which is the effect. Then, think of a cause or effect that has the same relationship to the last word.**

1. sleep : rested :: _____ : tired

2. look : see :: _____ : hear

3. close : zip :: _____ : unzip

4. run : escape :: _____ : catch

5. understand : decided :: _____ : uncertain

6. amusement : laugh :: _____ : cry

7. work : earn :: _____ : spend

8. taste : eat :: _____ : touch

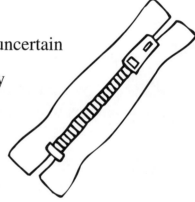

(GO ON ⇨)

The Third Word

Directions Read the words in the first word pair. Decide which is the cause and which is the effect. Then, think of a cause or effect that has the same relationship to the last word.

9. gas pedal : go :: _____ : stop

10. sweat : hot :: _____ : cold

11. fire : warm :: _____ : cold

12. fall : hurt :: _____ : heal

13. practice : improve :: _____ : learn

14. bend : break :: _____ : fix

15. rust : stick :: _____ : slide

16. disagree : argue :: _____ : cooperate

Analogy-Wiz

Write a cause and effect analogy, leaving out the third word. Put your analogy into a bowl or hat along with the analogies written by the rest of the class. Form two teams with the class. The teams should alternate, having a different person take one analogy from the hat or bowl and reading it aloud. The team can help with suggestions as to how to complete the analogy. When the team is ready, the person who chose the analogy reads it aloud. The other team may agree or disagree whether it is a true analogy. If it is true, your team gets a point.

The First Word

To complete these analogies, you will need to supply the first word. These analogies are a mix of different types of analogies. They may compare in many different ways.

Look at this example:

_____ : reaction :: turn : return

Think: What is the relationship between the words in the second word pair? **Return** is **turn** with the prefix **re** added. What is the root word of **reaction**?

Answer: Action is the root word of **reaction**, so **action** completes this analogy.

Now look at this example:

_____ : balm :: harsh : marsh

Think: What is the relationship between the words in the second word pair? **Harsh** and **marsh** are words that rhyme. What is a word that rhymes with **balm**?

Answer: Palm is a word that rhymes with **balm**, so **palm** is one word that can complete this analogy. (Other rhyming words would also complete this analogy.)

(Directions) Read the second word pair of each analogy. Decide what the relationship is between the two words. Complete the analogy with a word that has the same relationship to the second word. These analogies may compare in many different ways, and there may be more than one correct answer.

1. _____ : odor :: trip : journey

2. _____ : led :: pain : pane

3. _____ : measure :: pulley : lift

4. _____ : liquid :: atmosphere : gas

5. _____ : granular :: flour : fine

GO ON ⇒

The First Word

(Directions) Read the second word pair of each analogy. Decide what the relationship is between the two words. Complete the analogy with a word that has the same relationship to the second word. These analogies may compare in many different ways, and there may be more than one correct answer.

6. _____ : educators :: students : learners

7. _____ : sphere :: box : cube

8. _____ : tailor :: money : banker

9. _____ : ascend :: fall : descend

10. _____ : book :: volume : encyclopedia

11. _____ : sentence :: number : equation

12. _____ : ocean :: astronomer : sky

13. _____ : emotion :: mind : thought

14. _____ : data :: file cabinet : papers

15. _____ : fact :: novel : fiction

16. _____ : assemble :: break : destroy

Analogy-Wiz

Write three analogies, leaving out the first word. On a separate sheet of paper, write your answers and what each analogy is comparing, or why it works. Trade unfinished analogies with a classmate. Complete your classmate's analogies, and write what the analogy is comparing. Then, together with your partner, compare your answers and what you wrote about each analogy. Was there more than one possible answer? Did you agree about what each analogy was comparing?

Job Search

Directions The words in this search are all related to different types of jobs, or occupations. The words may run forward, backward, or diagonally. There may be more than one word that completes each analogy, but there is only one that can both complete the analogy and be found in the search. Your answers must do both.

1. farmer : tractor :: police officer : _____

2. stars : astronomer :: _____ : weather forecaster

3. lumber : _____ :: film : photographer

4. _____ : doctor :: school : teacher

5. sheep : _____ :: cattle : rancher

6. net : fisher :: _____ : cowboy

7. flippers : diver :: tap shoes : _____

8. _____ : soccer player :: court : tennis player

```
x  s  r  k  o  q  a  b  n  p  m
m  a  c  u  l  s  t  r  b  c  f
r  e  n  s  p  o  m  r  o  r  t
p  i  n  e  b  r  o  s  n  d  c
h  v  c  r  u  i  s  e  r  a  x
k  z  d  w  i  a  p  e  y  n  e
u  y  e  r  l  r  h  m  n  c  q
f  i  e  l  d  p  e  n  e  e  v
a  b  l  e  e  s  r  b  o  r  t
o  o  b  h  r  d  e  n  e  t  s
h  o  s  p  i  t  a  l  b  o  y
```

Analogies
Grades 4–5

Answer Key

page 3
forest; part of a whole
foot; where it's worn
brother; male relative

pages 4–5
1. distant; antonyms
2. passed; homophones
3. time; rhymes
4. discover; synonyms
5. map; parts of a whole
6. clothing; parts of a whole
7. feel; cause and effect
8. choir; parts of a whole
9. play; antonyms
10. mislead; synonyms
11. there; homophones
12. lever; rhymes
13. ending; antonyms
14. amazing; synonyms
15. gifted; synonyms
16. senses; parts of a whole
17. chill; cause and effect
18. rode; homophones

pages 6–7
Explanations, when required,
may vary slightly.
1. B. cube; describes shapes
2. C. chill; describes what its
    effect is
3. B. tough; describes its
    strength
4. A. able; describes ability
5. C. soothe; cause and effect
6. B. ocean / blue; describes
    color
7. B. medicine / bitter;
    describes taste
8. C. cottage / small; describes
    size
9. A. boulder / still; describes
    action
10. B. old / stale; describes
    quality
11. C. purely; adds suffix "ly"
12. C. 25; add 5
13. A. better; one degree
    difference
14. C. 300; multiply by 3
15. B. cool; compares most to
    least
16. C. he / his; grammatical
    equivalents
17. C. happy / happier; add
    suffix "er"
18. A. 48 / 12; divide by 4
19. B. close / disclose; add
    prefix "dis"
20. C. big / huge; compares one
    size up

pages 8–9
Answers may vary. Suggested
answers:
1. music; parts of a whole
2. girl; comparable gender
3. bear; where it lives
4. cows; how they travel
5. seedling or plant; next in
    sequence
6. build; what a person does
7. play; action
8. drive; what we do with it
9. round (or other shape); parts
    of a whole
10. evening or night; time of
    day
11. game; what it is
12. track; where it is done
13. mother; comparable relative
14. water; what it is
15. predator; what it is
16. start; synonyms
17. bite; sequence of events
18. goal; where the ball goes
19. words; what it is used for
20. inches; what it measures
21. Earth; what it revolves
    around
22. bedroom; where it is done
23. lion (or other mammal); its
    animal group
24. toe; parts of a whole

pages 10–11
1. sorrow; antonyms
2. dry; synonyms
3. evening; synonyms
4. destroy; synonyms
5. remain; synonyms
6. strength; antonyms
7. untrue; synonyms
8. success; antonyms
9. threat; synonyms
10. spectacular; antonyms
11. huge; synonyms
12. serious; synonyms

pages 12–13
1. flew; homophone
2. clasp; rhyme
3. harden; rhyme
4. tale; homophone
5. nickel; rhyme
6. flounder; rhyme
7. board; homophone
8. allowed; homophone
9. thunder; rhyme
10. heaven; rhyme

pages 14–15
1–15 show relationship of parts
to a whole; more specific
descriptions may follow
answers.
1. coyote; coverings
2. downtown; where it would
    be found
3. leg
4. book
5. tree
6. elephant
7. sled
8. shirt
9. automobile
10. television
11. pen
12. couch
13. sentence
14. century
15. galaxy
Analogy-Wiz:
human
ship
thermometer

pages 16–17
All show cause and effect
relationships.
1. dry
2. soothe
3. earn
4. weakness
5. distrust
6. confusion
7. tornado
8. calm
9. tears
10. wither
11. cure
12. escape
Analogy-Wiz:
hesitation
lose
still

page 18
Down:
1. bashful
3. silent
4. rinse
5. shelf
7. two or too
Across:
2. serious
6. punishment
8. solutions

pages 19–20
1. sphere; shapes
2. rounded; edges
3. dull; appearances
4. smooth; surfaces
5. quiet; sounds
6. humid; climates
7. wide; appearances
8. high; elevations
9. fleet; speeds
10. rough; surfaces
11. shallow; depths
12. smooth; effect on person
13. bland; tastes
14. gritty; feeling
15. light; weights

pages 21–22
All compare different degrees of
each characteristic.
1. terrified
2. starving
3. tiny
4. close
5. priceless
6. happy
7. ridiculous
8. tasty
9. evil
10. unbelievable
11. pretty
12. analyze
13. genius
14. bawl
15. happy
Analogy-Wiz:
Answers may vary.
worst
tiny
awesome

pages 23–24
All should be grammatically
comparable.
1. C. his
2. A. yours
3. C. run
4. B. wavier
5. C. brought
6. B. their
7. A. dancer
8. A. sat
9. B. painting
10. B. hers
11. B. driving
12. A. were
13. C. wettest
14. C. ran
15. B. discuss
16. C. brighten

pages 25–26
1. B. 15; add 1
2. C. 15; multiply by 3
3. A. 58; add 5
4. B. 25; divide by 2
5. A. 19; subtract 14
6. A. 12; multiply by 4
7. B. 2; add 2
8. C. 1; add 0 or multiply by 1
9. A. 60; add 10
10. C. 500; multiply by 2
11. C. 99; add 0 or multiply by 1
   Or B. 0; multiply by 0
12. A. 12; divide by 6

page 27
Answer listed first, other word shown in ( ).
1. creative (painter)
2. them (there)
3. thirty-three (nine)
4. several (none)
5. nimble (tall)
6. five (six)
7. talons (swift)
8. eleven (twelve)
Mystery answer: scramble

pages 28–29
1. d; people
2. e; space
3. f; one of a group/work together
4. b; how animals live
5. a; animal families
6. c; members of a group/professionals
7. k; space
8. g; kitchen items
9. m; how animals live
10. h; animal families
11. j; types of foods
12. o; sports related
13. p; specific uses
14. i; earth materials
15. n; foods
16. l; building locations

pages 30–31
1. snake : slither; how they move
2. toucan : rain forest; where they live
3. bear : hibernate; how they survive
4. bee : hive; where they live
5. lion : carnivore; what they eat
6. deer : forest; where they live
7. bison : plains; where they live
8. bird : feathers; coverings
9. snake : venom; how they protect themselves
10. walrus : tusks; how they fight
11. rhinoceros : horn; how they protect themselves
12. walrus : arctic; where they live
13. toad : hibernate; how they survive
14. swarm : bee; how they travel
15. eagle : speed; how they catch prey

pages 32–33
1. scissors : cut
2. moon : glow
3. towel : dry
4. red : stop
5. ice : preserve
6. heat : warm
7. professor : instruct
8. saw : cut
9. mystery : solve
10. rolling pin : roll
11. ship : carry
12. umbrella : protect
13. pencil : write
14. pedal : press

pages 34–35
1. A. chef : cook; what they do
2. C. astronomer : sky; what they study
3. A. master : teach; what they do
4. B. spider : trap; how they catch prey
5. A. bell : chime; sound they make
6. B. thriller : fright; emotion they evoke
7. C. lawyer : defend; what they do
8. A. farmer : crops; what they work with
9. B. photographer: photos; what they make
10. C. salt : season; what they do

page 36
1. d; tools
2. j; age/communication
3. h; how they communicate
4. g; sound they make
5. i; uses for books
6. f; town utilities
7. a; where or what they perform
8. c; what they measure
9. b; their use
10. e; household uses

page 37
1. bird : flock
2. desert rat : desert
3. strings : strum
4. cookie : dessert
5. corn : husk
6. bed : lie

pages 38–39
Answers may vary. All deal with sequence.
1. depart or leave
2. evening or night
3. run
4. unpack
5. eat
6. cow
7. succeed, understand, teach
8. Saturday
9. swallow
10. hold, take
11. cry
12. move
13. September
14. mend or discard
15. drink

pages 40–41
Answers may vary.
1. color
2. parent
3. game
4. scary
5. vegetable
6. gas
7. ocean
8. planet
9. round
10. wild
11. dog
12. grain
13. plant
14. insect
15. sense

pages 42–43
Answers may vary.
1. work
2. listen
3. open
4. chase
5. confused
6. sorrow
7. buy
8. feel
9. brake pedal
10. shiver
11. snow or ice
12. bandage
13. study
14. straighten
15. oil
16. agree

pages 44–45
Answers may vary.
1. smell; synonyms
2. lead; homophones
3. ruler; use
4. water; properties
5. salt, sand; texture
6. teachers; synonyms
7. ball; shapes
8. fabric; tools of the trade
9. climb; synonyms
10. chapter; parts of a whole
11. word; parts of a whole
12. oceanographer; what they study
13. heart; what we use (figuratively)
14. disk; types of storage
15. textbook or nonfiction; types of books
16. build; synonyms

page 46
1. cruiser
2. atmosphere
3. builder
4. hospital
5. shepherd
6. lasso
7. dancer
8. field

```
x s r k o q a b n p m
m a c u l s t r b c f
r e n s p o m r o r t
p i n e b r o s n d c
h v c r u i s e r a x
k z d w i a p e y n e
u y e r l r h m n c q
f i e l d p e n e e v
a b l e e s r b o r t
o o b h r d e n e t s
h o s p i t a l b o y
```